101 Tips and Tricks for Christian Writers

REBEKAH ARIAS

BloomWrite

FIRST EDITION

101 Tips and Tricks for Christian Writers

ISBN: 979-8-218-49482-7

Printed in the United States.

To Satu, who spreads sunshine wherever she goes.

Introduction

Introduction

Perhaps, like me, your childhood also included telltale signs—the prize you won in elementary school for a short story, the box of diaries stashed in your closet, or a report card comment: " . . . has a habit of daydreaming." Maybe you also devoured a book a day, rapidly depleting your small-town library's supply of fresh books. The budding writer in you may have showed up in other ways—a way with words or an ability to observe the world in minute detail.

Chances are, you've picked up this book because of that irresistible urge to capture beauty, tenderness, pain, or knowledge in words. You've accepted that you write in your head, think in stories, or see life as a series of scenes. You've accepted the calling. I've written this book with you in mind—I pray it will make your gift bloom.

Love, Rebekah

"Write down the revelation and make it plain" (Habakkuk 2:2).

1

Pause the Rollercoaster

Your laptop is open; your coffee is hot—time to write. Ten minutes pass, and you're still staring at the blank screen: writer in the headlights. Don't worry—there's a simple solution: Stop writing each day when you *least* want to. Think of it as pausing a rollercoaster at the crest of a hill. When you get to work the next day, you'll have plenty of momentum to keep going.

2

Be Stylish

Becoming familiar with the conventions of writing is essential. *The Christian Writer's Manual of Style* is a must read.

Although it may feel tedious, learning the conventions makes writing and self-editing easier (oh, and your editor will thank you too!).

3

Create a Writing Routine

I won't lie. The word *routine* is enough to make this creative break out in a rash. But I've come to understand that if I don't carve out a writing niche, it'll never happen. Having a routine helps prioritize what's important. I encourage you to find your own pocket—after work in the evenings, during your lunch break, after prayer time in the mornings, or before the family gets up, for example.

4

Be Self-Motivated

When I was nine, my class went on a field trip to the library to hear a children's author speak. Her talk must have been pretty enthralling, because halfway through it, I decided to become a writer. "What advice would you give aspiring authors?" I ventured. Her response has stuck with me to this day: "No one is going to tell you to write."

5

Let the Holy Spirit Lead You

Anyone can write a book. But not everyone writes with the Holy Spirit's guidance—that's a unique privilege given to Christian writers. Learn to partner with the Holy Spirit as you write, asking him to lead your thoughts and words. Fill yourself with the Word and listen more than you write.

6

Prayer Cures Writer's Block

Burn out. Fear. Perfectionism. Fatigue. Writer's block can strike for a number of reasons. When you find yourself stuck, pray. Ask God to reveal the blockage and give you a strategy. If he tells you to rest, rest. If he tells you to press on, press on. "He who began a good work in you will carry it on to completion" (Philippians 1:6).

7

Outlining Is Important

P age-long paragraphs, ideas that don't flow, repetition—all these point to structural issues. Even if you are a pantser (write by the seat of your pants) rather than a plotter (plan in meticulous detail), a basic outline is essential. Start big when writing an outline (chapter titles), then add more details (subheadings, bullet points).

8

Work with a Reputable Publisher

Whether you choose traditional or self-publishing, thoroughly investigate your options beforehand. There are thousands of publishing companies out there, but unfortunately, not all are scrupulous. Beware of vanity presses—publishing houses an author pays to publish their book, surrendering significant rights in the process. In many cases, you—not the reader—are the customer here.

9

Weed out Filler Words

Carina wished that Sam would speak up. Carina wished ~~that~~ Sam would speak up. That's better. When you edit, weed out as many filler words as possible—*that, literally, very, basically, interestingly,* etc. If a phrase keeps its meaning without it, it goes. Also, be mindful of idiosyncratic words you may be overusing.

10

Vary Your Syntax

I magine attending a concert where the orchestra plays the same melody over and over. You'd be bored in no time. Readers feel the same when reading a book with repetitive syntax. You can liven up your composition by varying transition words (*and, because, however*) and breaking up clusters of longer sentences with short, punchy ones.

11

Be Accountable

If you haven't done so already, get a writing buddy—someone who'll ask, "How much did you write this week?" (better still, someone who'll give you a kick in the seat of the pants when you need it!) While your accountability partner doesn't have to be a writer, it's helpful if they are. That way, you can encourage each other to achieve your respective writing goals.

12

Get Feedback, Get Beta

It's scary, I know. Handing over your newborn for scrutiny is a valuable yet gut-wrenching exercise. Reviews from friends and family members are helpful, but ultimately, you should look for someone you don't know. One way to find unbiased beta readers is to network with other writers on social media.

13

Find the Write Time

Whether you're a night owl or an early bird, find your most productive time and commit to it. Consistency is key. If you change your time slot too often, you'll lose momentum and risk falling off the wagon altogether. Start small and increase your writing time as you gain traction.

14

Bored Writer = Bored Reader

If you find your writing boring, your readers probably will too. Thankfully, you can make a mundane passages more interesting in a couple of simple ways. Break up large chunks of information, such as teaching, with anecdotes and condense long explanations. Keep paragraphs short—the visual break will allow the reader's eyes to rest.

15

Avoid Clichéd Tropes

Sadly, faith-based books and movies have a reputation for clichéd tropes. You know the ones: Every atheist in the story ends up converting, or all the character's problems disappear after they become a Christian. If you want to keep your reader guessing, dare to confront the complexities and paradoxes of real life.

16

Craft Flawed Characters

People are flawed. The Bible is full of them. When we create a perfect character, we carve out a beautiful yet lifeless statue, emotionally distancing the reader. Readers want to grapple with living, breathing characters—people who wrestle with their vulnerabilities, break, fall, and get back up again—just like them.

17

Set Up a Designated Workspace

J ane Austen balanced her writing atop a tiny walnut nightstand. While this setup obviously won't work for your desktop computer, there's a lot to be said for a designated writing space. It doesn't have to be fancy—a small comfy nook will do. Invest in your posture with an ergonomic chair and an adjustable laptop stand. The stand will raise your eye-level, preventing neck and shoulder pain.

18

Look after Your Body

Let's face it: Writing is a workout for the fingers and the mind but not much else. Throw in unhealthy snacking and late-night writing sessions, and it's a recipe for health issues. You can protect your longevity in ministry (yes, writing is a ministry) and boost productivity by staying active, eating right, and getting enough sleep. Small choices make a big difference in the long run.

19

Change Is as Good as a Holiday

You can also increase your productivity with a change in your scenery. Getting out and about may just give you the inspiration you need—you might encounter a quirky librarian who ends up in your novel or discover your creativity percolates better in the busy buzz of a coffee shop.

20

Connect with Your Reader

My favorite nonfiction books feel like a catch-up over coffee—the author addresses the reader directly in a conversational tone. What's your favorite nonfiction book? How does the author's tone affect their delivery? Do you feel the author genuinely cares about you, the reader? Why? Asking questions like these will improve your writing and help you connect with your audience.

21

Be Faithful to the Word

In Deuteronomy 4:12, Moses exhorts the Israelites not to add or subtract anything from God's Word. This is a healthy reminder for Christian writers to filter everything we say through the lens of Scripture. Our writing doesn't have to scream Bible, but if we scratch the surface, it should at least bleed Bible.

22

Cite It, Don't Just Write It

A barrage of unsubstantiated facts is like an empty promise. Citing your sources tells the reader you've done your due diligence—they can believe what you say with confidence. If you wrestle with citations like me, you may find the citation features in Microsoft Word and Scrivener helpful.

23

Ditch Imposter Syndrome

When I left my regular job to minister and write full time, I often felt like a fraud. I would sit at my desk thinking, *Am I really a writer, or am I just playacting*? Then one day, God popped an idea into my head. I ordered a colorful nameplate with "author" inscribed under my name and put it on my desk—a reminder of God's calling. I encourage you to get your own reminder, one that speaks to you.

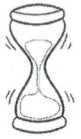

24

Take Frequent Breaks

D o you want to be more productive? Good news: you don't have to spend more time writing with fewer breaks—just the opposite. Take shorter, more frequent breaks, and you'll actually increase your output. Try taking a five-to-ten-minute break every hour to stretch, walk around the block, or grab a healthy snack. It'll get your blood pumping, stave off boredom, and clear your head.

25

Get Tough on Distractions

Her name is Audrey, and I bought her to combat the distractions of modern life. That jaunty little 1960s Corona typewriter did her best for a few weeks—until my fingers hurt, and I got frustrated making mistakes. Today, she mostly writes invitations and amuses my kids (I've discovered turning off my phone is far more productive). What helps you give writing your full attention?

26

Practice Makes Perfect

Learning another language is wonderful medicine if you're a perfectionist. It forces you to make mistakes, correct them, and carry on (I've accidentally said some things in Spanish that still make me blush!) Writing is the same. You'll churn out mediocre work from time to time as you learn. It's okay. It's supposed to happen. Don't beat yourself up—the fact you're recognizing and correcting mistakes means you're learning.

27

Do Your Market Research

When you decide what book to write, it pays to do your homework. Is there a market for the book? Is it a broad market or a niche one? What books already exist like the one you plan to write? If the market's already saturated, does your book offer a unique perspective? If it doesn't, you may want to reconsider writing it or look for a different angle. Partner your research with prayer.

28

Know Why You Write

"Why do you write?" The blunt question caught me off guard. How was this related to my complaint in an online writer's group about struggling to finish a book? I wrote and deleted a half-dozen replies before posting. The response appeared almost right away: "Then write." Finally, I understood the stranger's cryptic message: Get on with it. If you know why you write, the how will follow.

29

Identify Your Target Audience

Identifying *who* you write for is almost as important as knowing *why* you write. What's your audience's age range? Are they male or female? Christian or non-Christian? Saying "My book is for everyone" is like shooting a bundle of arrows and hoping they all hit the target. Ask yourself, "What specific problem does a particular group have that my book can solve?"

30

Avid Readers Make Great Writers

Read often—all different genres and styles. Read the classics, bestsellers, and some that aren't so great. Put on your writer glasses and pull apart the author's style and use of techniques. Analyze why a book is a gem or a lemon and use those observations to improve your writing.

31

Take Note

B esides being a voracious reader, be a keen observer. When our family ministered in Europe for three weeks, I filled two notebooks with impressions of the people and places we visited. For now, those journals are marinating in a closet, waiting patiently for the right project. Make a habit of carrying a notebook everywhere, and you can capture snippets of life while they are fresh.

32

Be a Royal Scribe

In ancient times, a royal scribe's job was to stay close to the king, listen to his words, and capture them. A Christian writer's responsibility is much the same: "Write down the revelation and make it plain" (Habakkuk 2:2). As you write, position yourself to hear from God. Ask him to align your imagination and abilities with his purposes.

33

Use Character Profiles

What are your characters' likes and dislikes? What are their backgrounds, hopes, fears, and dreams? What makes them tick, and what keeps them awake at night? A character profile, often used by actors to help get into character, can help answer these questions. Profiles also make it easier to craft well-rounded characters who respond to situations in believable ways.

34

Copyright Is King

As writers, particularly *Christian* writers, we should take copyright seriously. This means taking specific legal steps: purchasing a commercial license to use an image or getting a person's permission to write about them by name. Do whatever integrity demands—it'll also save you a lot of headaches later on.

35

Invest in a Professional Cover

It's true. Readers often judge a book by the cover. If you're self-publishing, it's worth investing the time, energy, and finances to create a standout cover. Avoid cliches, e.g. love-hearts on a book about relationships, outdated fonts, and visual clutter. If you decide to design your own cover, be honest about the results. When in doubt, hire a professional.

36

Write Humbly

I cringed. The pamphlet I held in my hands practically screamed, "Atheists are stupid." If I were an atheist, it would go straight into the trash (note: it still went in the trash). Whether your target audience is Christian or non-Christian, avoid writing in a preachy, condescending tone. Communicate the truth in love and humility instead.

37

A Great Title Sells

Your book needs an eye-catching cover and snappy title. The title should be concise, between three and five words at the most (if you need to explain further, add a subtitle). It should reveal the premise of the book without giving it away completely—you don't want a potential reader to know the entire plot just by looking at the cover.

38

Investigate before You Publish

Self-, hybrid, or traditional publishing? Before you commit, you'll want to ask a few questions: How much does self-publishing cost? Is the hybrid publisher truly hybrid or a vanity publisher? What's in the contract's fine print? If you traditionally publish, you will probably need an agent, which can be a challenge when you don't have a strong platform. If still aren't sure, remember, you can always self-publish if traditional publishing doesn't materialize.

39

Set the Mood

You don't need a lake house or a cabin in the woods to create a cozy writing retreat. Sprinkle your workspace with items you love to create the same effect. My go-tos are candles that sound crackling logs on a fire and fresh flowers. Think about what you love—art, sports, music, history, or other items. Choose objects that will lift your mood without distracting you.

40

Writing Is a Marathon, Not a Sprint

"Three days in a hotel room, and I *will* finish my book!" My family knew the refrain well. Life got busy, the retreat never materialized, and I stopped writing. Several months later, a total stranger sent me this message on my birthday: "Write a little each day, and it will get done." I took the word from the Lord to heart and got back to work. If you write a little each day and are consistent, your manuscript *will* grow—slowly but surely.

41

Creativity Doesn't Exist in a Vacuum

The founding fathers of Impressionism worked together closely, playing off each other's strengths, ideas, and innovations. They understood that creativity doesn't exist in a vacuum—it's fueled by outside influences. The best way to get your creative juices flowing is to immerse yourself in others' work, preferably across a variety of disciplines.

42

Embrace Editing

Love it or hate it—editing is the most important stage of writing. American mystery writer Phyllis A. Whitney observed, "Good stories are not written; they are re-written."[1] In other words, your first draft won't be wonderful. You have to *make* it wonderful. Skimping on self-editing will leave your book half-baked—and you can't expect your editor to fix that.

---

1. Phyllis A. Whitney, *Writing juvenile stories and novels : how to write and sell fiction for young people* (Boston: The Writer, 1976), 126.

43

Writing Has Eternal Value

"*What if books become obsolete?*" I fretted one day. God's gentle response to my pseudo-prayer brought tears to my eyes: "Books will never pass away. They are important in heaven, and they are important to me." He understood the question behind my question: "Does what I'm doing matter?" If you have ever asked this question, be encouraged—your writing has eternal value.

44

Shop Around for a Printer

When choosing a printer, price, quality, and book size are important considerations for a self-published author. Most companies print standard book sizes, whereas a custom size usually narrows your printer options and costs more. The most common standard book sizes are six by nine inch (fiction) and five and a half by eight and a half inch (nonfiction).

45

Scams Are Everywhere

Here are some ways you can protect yourself from writing scams:

1. Be cautious if a publisher chases you to publish your work.

2. Do an online search of the publisher's name, adding the word "scam."

3. Read as many reviews of the publisher as possible.

4. Look out for inflated fees, split royalties, and over-promising.

46

Balance the "Me" in Memoir

Even though a memoir is *your* story, write with your reader in mind. How will your story benefit the reader and connect with their own story? Craft a memoir that feels like a two-way conversation, rather than a monologue. An effective writer doesn't just write well; they write with empathy.

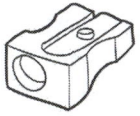

47

Write Fearlessly

T he purpose of a first draft is to slap down your initial ideas, like clay on a wheel. Don't think. Just get it all down. Once your first draft is complete, then it's time to mold and refine your manuscript. Editing as you go along is ~~counterproductive~~ like trying to glaze raw pottery while it's still wet and spinning.

48

Inspiration Comes Through Writing

Feeling uninspired? Write. Can't settle on the perfect way to begin? Just write. Want to get unstuck? You've got it—write. The spark of inspiration often strikes *as* we write, not before. Always remember that writing is a discipline, not a feeling.

49

Take Advantage of Technology

Today, a myriad of programs and apps are available to assist writers. Stuck on editing? Grammarly or ProWritingAid can help. If you want to design your own book cover, Adobe Express is a user-friendly tool. For interior formatting, InDesign is the leading software for publishing design (the learning curve can be steep, however, depending on your prior experience).

50

Make Your Back Cover Sing

A back cover often includes a short biography and summary, also called the blurb. The purpose of the biography is to build credibility—it shows your reader you know what you're talking about. Depending on the tone of your book, the biography can be serious or lighthearted. Children's authors, for example, often include a funny fact about themselves. A blurb should be short enough to hold a potential reader's attention and long enough to capture the book's essence.

51

Get a Professional Headshot

A headshot should be high resolution, in focus, and natural-looking. Avoid wearing busy patterns and clashing colors, and consider the look and image you want to project (style, facial expression). Use natural lighting and a simple background. A high-quality phone camera may do the trick; if not, seek out a professional photographer.

52

Hire a Professional Editor

Asking a friend to edit your book may seem convenient, but unless that friend is a professional, it's risky business. You should approach freelance marketplaces with similar caution. A legitimate editor will usually have a website with samples and be open to discussing their qualifications. If you're not sure where to start, the Christian Editor Connection is a free service that connects authors with qualified, established editors.

53

Invest in Professional Learning

There are many ways to grow as a writer. You could attend a writer's retreat, get a writing certificate through a college, or take advantage of online masterclasses from experienced writers, such as Jerry B. Jenkins, the bestselling author of the Left Behind series. Jenkins has a treasure-trove of YouTube tutorials and resources available online.

54

Use Hooks

"All children, except one, grow up." The opening line of J.M. Barrie's *Peter Pan* is a great example of a hook—an attention-grabbing statement that generates unanswered questions. *Who doesn't grow up?* we wonder. *And why don't they grow up—how is that even possible?* We must read the rest of the book to find out.

55

Develop Your Characters

A character arc is a character's inner journey. It unfolds when you're willing, like a good parent, to take a step back and let your protagonist make mistakes. Antagonists also evolve, albeit to a lesser extent. While they don't necessarily have to become good, your villains should move closer or further away from their goals. You may find it useful to map out each character's arc in the beginning.

56

Try, Try, Try Again

When you pour your heart and soul into a book for months, even years, rejections can be incredibly disheartening. But don't give up. Refine your manuscript or proposal and try, try, try again. If you feel discouraged, remember publishers rejected *Gone with the Wind* thirty-eight times!

57

Marketing Matters

Marketing. Most authors hate it. But even if you work with a traditional publisher, you'll still have to participate in the promotion of your book. An author website with a recognizable brand is a great place to start. You can also engage readers with a video, connect with a local bookstore, experiment with paid advertisements, or do a book giveaway.

58

Show, Don't Tell

"Show, don't tell" is a narrative technique that uses sensory details to paint a picture in the reader's mind, rather than spell out the action. I could tell you that "Hayden felt overwhelmed with anger," or I could describe how "Hayden's clenched fists burned." Both sentences convey the same idea, but the second example allows the reader to think for themselves.

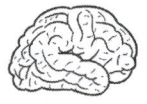

59

Write What You Know…Sort Of

Mark Twain is thought to have said, "Write what you know." But what if you write sci-fi or fantasy? What if you've never been to outer space or traveled to a lost city? J.R. Tolkien spent twelve years writing *Lord of the Rings* and creating Middle Earth, complete with its own culture and languages. In his case it could be said, "Write what you know—discover what you don't."

60

Use Active Voice

A simple way to improve your writing is to use active voice. In passive voice, the subject is acted upon: "The stick is chased by a dog." In active voice, the subject performs an action: "The dog chases a stick." Active voice engages the reader and pulls them into the story. It also makes it easier for the reader to comprehend the action, following the subject-verb-object structure our brains are accustomed to.

61

Don't Head-Hop

Head hopping occurs when the point of view bounces between the inner thoughts and feelings of multiple characters. This confuses the reader, making it difficult to know who the focal character is. The only exception to this rule is omniscient point of view, also called the God-perspective. In omniscient, the narrator is not actively involved in the plot.

62

Use Consistent Tenses

A change in tenses is jarring for the reader. For example, "The professor *launched* into a lengthy explanation, unaware that most of his students *fall* asleep." In this sentence, the verbs switch from past to present tense. If you aren't sure, read your writing aloud—if something doesn't sound right, it probably isn't.

63

Craft Punchy Prose

Earnest Hemingway once said, "If a writer of prose knows enough about what he is writing about, he may omit things that he knows and the reader . . . will have a feeling of those things as strongly as though the writer had stated them."[1] Hemingway understood that prose doesn't have to capture every single detail, like a photograph. A skilled writer can paint vivid imagery using only a few broad strokes. He trusts the reader to fill in the blanks.

---

1. Ernest Hemingway, *Death in the Afternoon* (New York: Charles Scribner's Sons, 1923), 192.

64

Create Realistic Dialogue

Dialogue should mimic everyday speech—without the boring bits. Take a real argument, for example. During a conflict, communication is heightened. People overlap and interrupt each other. You can recreate this sense of immediacy by removing arbitrary greetings and small talk from your dialogue. If it doesn't create intrigue or advance the plot, it goes.

65

Use Dialogue Tags Sparingly

A dialogue tag should be simple, inconspicuous, and used only where necessary. If you use adverbs, e.g., "he hissed *angrily*", try to keep them to a minimum (less than 10 percent is a good target). Too many -ly adverbs indicate you are telling rather than showing. *Said* is nearly invisible and is sufficient for most dialogue tags.

66

Turn Pages with Setups and Payoffs

Readers love surprises—a fact Agatha Christie skillfully exploited. Like Christie, you can use setups and payoffs to keep readers turning pages. Setups are events that create questions in the reader's mind. Payoffs answer those questions, often in unexpected ways. Omit setups that have no follow-through. You might find it helpful to write your setups and payoffs in reverse.

67

Just Say It

Mellifluous and abstruse disquisition will indubitably rankle your reader. You get the idea. Inflating your writing with long jargon—unless you're writing for scholarly or legal purposes—doesn't make for enjoyable reading. As C.S. Lewis said, "Always prefer the plain, direct word to the long, vague one."[1]

---

1. C.S. Lewis, *Letters of C. S. Lewis,* ed. W. H. Lewis (London: Geoffrey Bles, 1966), 271.

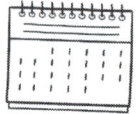

68

Embrace the Day of Small Beginnings

After years of hard work, launch day is here—it's time to present your newborn to the world. You hold your book aloft, Lion King–style, and wait for the masses to realize this is the one they've been waiting for their whole lives. At the end of the evening, you discover a grand total of six people purchased a copy—mostly family members. If this has happened to you, please don't get discouraged. The day of small beginnings is just that—a beginning! (Zechariah 4:10).

69

Establish an Author Platform

An author platform is an important consideration for publishers. It speaks of your influence and your ability to reach a target audience. If the idea of self-promotion makes you uncomfortable, it may be helpful to think in terms of promoting the message God has entrusted you with, rather than promoting yourself.

70

Write Often

Writing is like going to the gym. If you do it every day, you'll stay motivated. Neglect writing for a few days, weeks, or months, and you'll gradually lose momentum and focus. If you need to step back, try to limit your break to a week or less, especially if you're working on a first draft.

71

Edit, Edit, Edit

Q: How many times should I edit a manuscript?

A: As many times as necessary.

The goal is to get your manuscript as close to perfect as possible. Be prepared to do multiple passes for readability, grammatical errors, citations, etc., and don't be surprised if editing takes much longer than writing your first draft. Not only is this normal, it's to be expected.

72

Set Goals

I like to keep a schedule of my writing goals on a pin-up board above my desk. Every check mark at the end of the day gives me a sense of satisfaction and energizes me. Setting a daily writing quota increases productivity because it breaks down your manuscript into smaller, manageable bites. Some writers find it helpful to write in short, timed sprints.

73

Watch Out for Rabbit Holes

R abbit holes are pointless side trips that have no bearing on a narrative. You can avoid them by ensuring your character's actions advance the plot or reveal something of their inner workings. If Tim and Sharon go to a wedding simply to enjoy themselves, for example, the exercise is wasted. But if something occurs there to reveal glimpses of their true feelings for one another, the wedding becomes a plot device. This applies to both events and dialogue: it must advance the story.

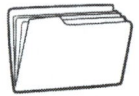

74

Know Your Publishing House's Requirements

Before you type a word, you'll want to know if the publishing house you've had your eye on accepts manuscripts or proposals only. Do they allow author submissions, or will you need a literary agent? (Many publishing houses won't look at a manuscript without an agent.) What are the requirements and conventions for genres, formatting, length, etc.?

75

Query Letters Attract Agents

A literary agent's job is to negotiate and secure author contracts with publishing houses. To acquire an agent, you'll need to write a convincing query letter. The letter should introduce your book, include a short bio, and be no longer than a page. Be sure to end by thanking the reader.

76

You Are Not Your Writing

Writing is intensely personal. Just as God created man in his image, your writing bears your unique imprint—your words and thoughts. But you are not your writing. If you've ever felt discouraged by criticism, just remember: Although your writing bears your stamp, you bear Christ's. Your identity is in him.

77

Eliminate Throat-Clearing

B abbling. Rambling. Throat-clearing. The purpose of a first draft is to get it out of your system. In subsequent drafts, weed out unnecessary backstories squeezed into dialogue or information dumps. Drop your reader into the action right away and reveal key information as the plot unfolds.

78

Make It Easy for People to Buy Your Books

Y ou're at a speaking engagement selling books. You have a QR code and change for those who want to pay in cash. The only problem is, not everyone trusts the security of QR codes or has cash on hand. Most people prefer to pay with a debit or credit card. The more payment options you offer, the more books you are likely to sell.

79

Balance Online Presence with Real-World Connections

For the introverted writer, the thought of being able to write, format, market, etc., online may sound wonderful—but it's only the beginning. To promote your book successfully, you'll need to forge real-world connections. Attending author events and networking with professionals in the publishing industry are highly recommended.

80

Edit Ruthlessly

Self-edit with the ferocity of a pirate commandeering a treasure ship. Take no prisoners—if something isn't working, make it walk the plank. Trust your intuition. If you sense a passage is dull or monotonous, it probably is. If you still aren't sure, get a second—or even a third—opinion.

81

Find Your Voice

I grew up on a steady diet of Austen, Alcott, and Montgomery—a fact that's blatantly obvious in a diary I wrote at twelve, chronicling my family's adventures across outback Australia ("alas, we were beset once more by engine troubles"). I eventually stopped imitating my heroes but still credit them with being my first writing mentors. Absorb classic writing while developing your unique voice.

82

Write Books You Would Like to Read

"I want one like this but with Bible ladies," my eldest daughter said, pointing to a book emblazoned with animated princesses. I pulled out my phone. "Let's have a look, honey." *There should be a ton of books like that*. Half an hour later, I was still searching. The book didn't seem to exist. "Why don't you write it, Mummy?" Miss Five asked. Four years later, I published "Twelve Bible Princesses." If there's a book you want to read that doesn't exist, write it.

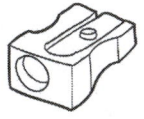

83

Don't Overuse Gerunds

When you pepper your writing with too many words that end in -ing, also called present participles or gerunds, it can sound wordy and weak. For example:

A. When you are taking pride in your work, you are doing your best.

B. When you take pride in your work, you do your best.

The second edited example is concise and projects confidence.

84

Edit With Your Reader Hat, Not Your Writer Hat

After I complete a first draft, I usually take a week-long break to reset my brain. I then print off a hard copy and force myself to read all the way through without editing (it's hard!) When I held the hard copy of the manuscript and read it with fresh eyes, I could switch my brain from writer to reader, which made it easier to spot problem areas.

85

Don't Cut Corners

You might be tempted to cut corners to save money, especially if you're on a tight budget, but it's not worth it. Shortcuts will ultimately hurt your credibility as an author, which could mean your target audience won't buy your subsequent books. It's better to take the time, spend the money, and do whatever is necessary to produce a quality product.

86

Format Your Book Properly

Mess up the formatting.

How do you ruin a book?

All jokes aside, unprofessional formatting is like wearing sweatpants to a job interview. No matter how wonderfully written a book is, readers notice poor presentation right away. If you plan on tackling the job yourself, you'll need to know the conventions for text justification, gutter sizing, paragraph indentations, and dialogue. Otherwise, hire a professional to do it correctly.

87

Go to the Source

The true mark of a royal scribe is time spent at the Master's feet. Everything else—editing, formatting, marketing, etc.—should come second. For our writing to bring people closer to God, we must first draw near to him. Revelation and relationship are inseparable.

88

Don't Sacrifice Family on the Altar of Ministry

Writing is an intense, solitary pursuit, requiring many sacrifices. One thing we should never sacrifice, however, is family. You can honor your loved ones by setting limits on your writing. Regularly take time to unplug, have fun, and be fully present. As with any ministry, balance is essential.

89

Give More than You Take

Generosity is an integral part of God's economy. A free give-away for your followers is a great way to reflect this culture of generosity. Create gifts that are genuinely useful—checklists, helpful hints, podcasts with no strings attached—and let your readers know how much you appreciate them.

90

Use Humor When Possible

T hink back to your high school days for a moment. Remember the class clown—that one student who had the entire class eating out of their hand? They understood the assignment: Humor creates engagement. Your writing doesn't have to read like a comedy routine, but even serious books can benefit from a smattering of humor.

91

Don't Preach to the Choir

Your reader should be able to tell who your target audience is within the first few pages of your book. If it's not clear, you might be trying to engage the wrong group. A book written for a non-Christian audience shouldn't include a lot of Christianese (Christian jargon), and a book for mature Christians doesn't need to explain the fundamentals of salvation.

92

Write for Your Audience of One

L et's face it, even if you turn out a literary masterpiece, it simply won't be everyone's flavor (hello, Shakespeare). That's why it's better to wait until a manuscript is almost complete before consulting beta readers. You'll avoid the temptation to alter your book to suit everyone—potentially spoiling it. Improve your craft, by all means, but ultimately write for your audience of one.

93

Read Your Work Aloud

C.S. Lewis said, "Always write (and read) with the ear, not the eye."[1] Reading your work aloud makes it easier to spot issues with sentence structure, flow, and readability. And if you don't feel up to reading all six hours of your manuscript, AI can help. The latest text-to-voice apps sound realistic and have largely lost their robotic quality.

---

1. Lewis, *Letters of C. S. Lewis,* 279.

94

Draw Inspiration from Real Life

Did you know Louisa M. Alcott tried her hand at sensational gothic fiction before penning the young adult classic *Little Women*? Like her protagonist, Jo March, Alcott realized her best inspiration came from real life—her three sisters. When you draw inspiration from real individuals and events, you infuse your writing with a sense of emotional authenticity.

95

Discover How You Write Best

Ernest Hemmingway wrote using a typewriter, standing up. Roald Dahl wrote in a garden shed, sitting in an enormous armchair. Bestselling American author James Patterson writes longhand in pencil. How do you write? Perhaps you alternate between sitting down and standing up or record voice notes while packing your kids' school lunches. There's no wrong way—find what works for you.

96

Keep Track of Your Ideas

I have a problem—I'm addicted to starting new books. About halfway through a first draft, I'll start following the siren song of a new project (unfinished manuscript count: currently five). If you also suffer from "shiny book syndrome," I recommend buying a ring-bound pack of index cards and recording each new idea on a separate card. That way, you can capture inspiration when it hits *and* focus on your current project.

97

Spiritual Warfare Is Real

Odd. Every time I sat down to do a final proofread, my children began to fight, household items broke, and mini-crises erupted. I was at my wit's end, until I heard God say, "Keep going. Soon, you'll understand." Two days after I completed my second book, a Christian publisher contacted me. What I initially thought was a scam turned out to be a doorway to distribution in the UK. When you face spiritual opposition, push through.

98

Aim for Excellence

Aren't you glad when God created the earth, he made it "very good," not just good enough? As Christian writers, we should never settle for good enough—the high standard of our work should reflect God's excellence. "Whatever you do, do it all for the glory of God" (1 Corinthians 10:31 NIV).

99

There Are Different Types of Editing

The stages of editing are like building a house. Developmental editing, also called structural editing, reinforces the house's frame. Copy editing deals with details inside the house—grammar, spelling, syntax, etc. The final stage, proofreading, completes the house, making it watertight or error-free).

100

Hire a Talented Illustrator

Children are visually wired. To give your self-published picture book the best chance of being read, hire a professional illustrator. Work out logistics like time frame, cost per illustration, and copyright beforehand. Give clear and concise feedback, and be open to your illustrator's input—the creative process works best as a partnership.

101

Writers Write

M any are called to write. But few embrace the challenge. The difference between being inspired to write and being a writer is that *writers write*. Don't worry about your qualifications or lack thereof—God always equips those he calls. Be willing to learn. Write.

Made in the USA
Columbia, SC
27 September 2024

43174732R00059